the Temptations
Greatest Hits

Cover photo by Michael Ochs Archives.com

ISBN 1-4234-1117-X

HAL•LEONARD®
CORPORATION

7777 W. BLUEMOUND RD. P.O. BOX 13819 MILWAUKEE, WI 53213

Visit Hal Leonard Online at
www.halleonard.com

the Contents

AIN'T TOO PROUD TO BEG

Words and Music by EDWARD HOLLAND
and NORMAN WHITFIELD

Moderately fast

I know you wan-na leave me, but I re-fuse to let you go.

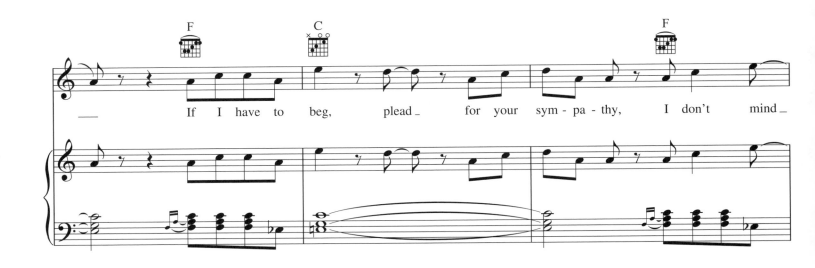

If I have to beg, plead for your sym-pa-thy, I don't mind

'cause you mean that much to me. Ain't too proud to beg, and you know it.
(Ooh, sweet dar-

BALL OF CONFUSION
(That's What the World Is Today)

Words and Music by NORMAN WHITFIELD
and BARRETT STRONG

Moderately slow

Peo-ple mov-in' out, peo-ple mov-in' in, why?___ Be - cause of the col - or of their skin,

run, run, run ___ but you sho' can't hide. ___ An

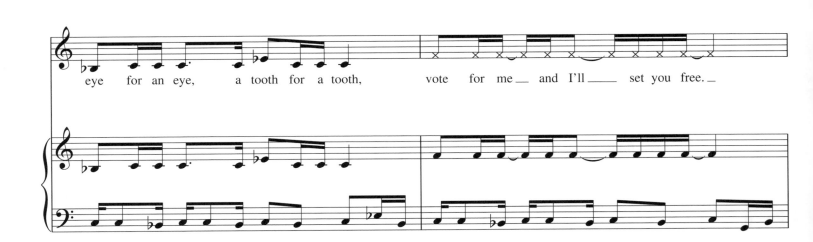

eye for an eye, a tooth for a tooth, vote for me ___ and I'll ___ set you free. ___

ball of con-fu - sion, __ oh __ yeah, __ that's what the world is to-day.

The sale of pills __ is at an all - time high,

young folks walk-in' 'round __ with their heads in the sky, __ cit-ies a - flame __ in the sum-mer-time, __ and oh __

__ the beat goes on. __

E - vo - lu - tion, re - vo - lu - tion, gun con - trol, the sound of soul, shoot - in' rock - ets to the moon, kids grow - ing up too soon.

Pol - i - ti - cians say more tax - es will solve ev -'ry - thing, and the band played

on.

Round and a - round and a - round we go where the world's head - ed no - bod - y knows. __

CLOUD NINE

Words and Music by BARRETT STRONG
and NORMAN WHITFIELD

Moderately, with double-time feeling

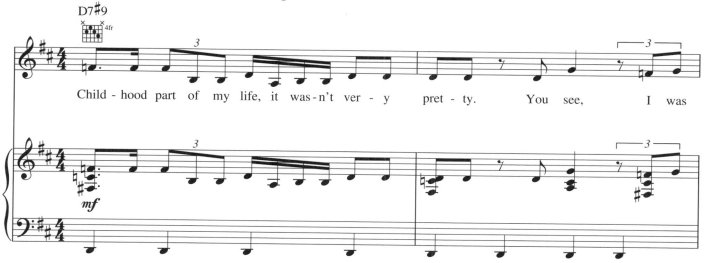

Child - hood part of my life, it was-n't ver - y pret - ty. You see, I was

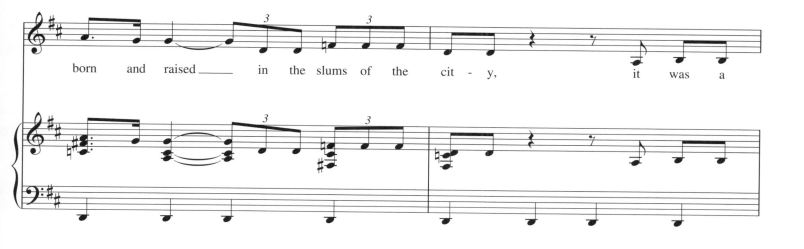

born and raised _____ in the slums of the cit - y, it was a

one room shack that slept ten oth - er chil - dren be - sides me. _____ We

BEAUTY IS ONLY SKIN DEEP

Words and Music by EDWARD HOLLAND
and NORMAN WHITFIELD

GET READY

Words and Music by
WILLIAM "SMOKEY" ROBINSON

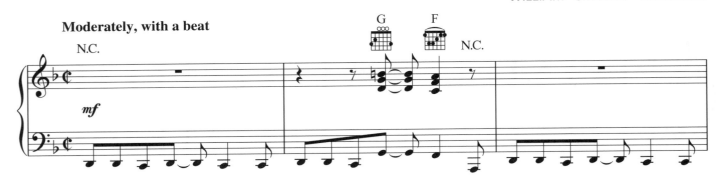

I nev-er met a girl who makes __ me feel __ the way that
wan-na play __ hide and seek __ with love, __ let me re-
All __ my __ friends should-n't want me to, __ I un-der-

you do. (It's al - right.) __ When-ev-er I'm asked __ who makes
mind you. (It's al - right.) __ The lov-ing you're gon - na miss,
stand it. (Be al - right.) __ I hope __ I'll get __ to you be-

I CAN'T GET NEXT TO YOU

Words and Music by BARRETT STRONG
and NORMAN WHITFIELD

Guitar solo

1. I can turn the
2., 3. *(See additional lyrics)*

grey sky blue ___ and I can make it rain ___ when-ev-er I want it to. ___ And

34

Additional Lyrics

2. I can fly like a bird in the sky
   And I can buy anything that money can buy.
   I can turn a river into a raging fire.
   I can live forever if I so desire.
   I don't want it, all these things I can do
   'Cause I can't get next to you.
   Chorus

3. I can turn back the hands of time — you better believe I can.
   I can make the seasons change just by waving my hand.
   I can change anything from old to new.
   The thing I want to do the most I'm unable to do.
   I'm an unhappy woman with all the powers I possess
   'Cause man, you're the key to my happiness.

I WISH IT WOULD RAIN

Words and Music by NORMAN WHITFIELD,
BARRETT STRONG and ROGER PENZABENE, SR.

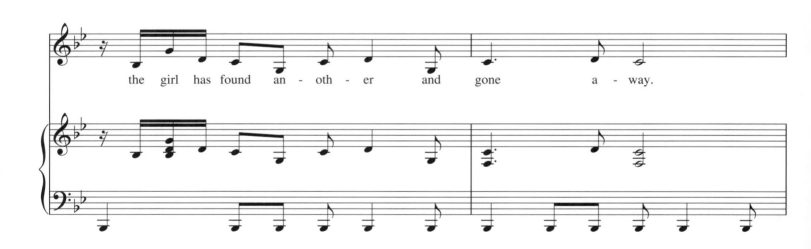

Additional Lyrics

2. 'Cause so badly I wanna go outside but everyone knows that a man ain't suppose to cry.
   Listen, I gotta cry 'cause crying eases the pain, oh yeah, people this hurt I feel inside,
   Words could never explain. I just wish it would rain.

3. Day in day out my tear-stained face pressed against the windowpane,
   My eyes search the skies desperately for rain, 'cause raindrops will hide my teardrops
   And no one will ever know that I'm crying, crying when I go outside.
   To the world outside my tears, I refuse to explain, oh I wish it would rain.

I'M LOSING YOU
(I Know)

Words and Music by CORNELIUS GRANT,
NORMAN WHITFIELD and EDWARD HOLLAND

Your love _____ is fad - in', I can feel your love fad - in'.

I'M GONNA MAKE YOU LOVE ME

Words and Music by LEON HUFF,
KENNETH GAMBLE and JERRY ROSS

JUST MY IMAGINATION
(Running Away with Me)

Words and Music by NORMAN J. WHITFIELD
and BARRETT STRONG

Each day through my win-dow I
Soon we'll be

watch her as she pass-es by. ___ I
mar-ried and raise a fam - i - ly. A

say to my-self, "You're such ___ a luck-y guy. ___
co-zy lit-tle home out in the coun-try with two chil-dren, may-be three.

MY GIRL

Words and Music by WILLIAM "SMOKEY" ROBINSON
and RONALD WHITE

I've got sun-shine

on a cloud - y day. ___

When it's

cold out - side, ___

I've ___ got the month of May. ___

58

PAPA WAS A ROLLIN' STONE

Words and Music by NORMAN WHITFIELD
and BARRETT STRONG

It was the third of Sep - tem - ber.
nev - er got a chance to see ___

That day I'll al - ways re - mem - ber, yes, I will, ___ 'cause
___ him. Nev - er heard noth - in' but bad things a - bout him.

THE WAY YOU DO THE THINGS YOU DO

Words and Music by WILLIAM "SMOKEY" ROBINSON
and ROBERT ROGERS

YOU'RE MY EVERYTHING

Words and Music by NORMAN WHITFIELD,
ROGER PENZABENE and CORNELIUS GRANT

Moderately

1. You sure-ly just know mag-ic, girl, _____ 'cause you changed my
2., 3. (See additional lyrics)

life.

It was dull ___ and or-di-nar-y,

but you make it sun-ny and bright.

Additional Lyrics

2. When my way was dark and troubles were near,
   Your love provided the light so I could see.
   Girl, just knowing your love was near when times were bad
   Kept the world from closing in on me, girl.
   I was blessed the day I found you; gonna build my whole world around you.
   You're everything good, girl, and you're all that matters to me.

3. Girl, you're the girl I sing about in every love song I sing.
   You're my winter, baby, my summer, my fall, my spring.
   I was blessed the day I found you; gonna build my whole world around you.
   You're everything good, girl, and you're all that matters to me.